CONTENTS

South Africa – An Overview

The Republic of South Africa is Africa's wealthiest economy. Occupying less than one-twentieth of the continent, it produces around 40 per cent of Africa's manufactured goods, nearly 50 per cent of its minerals and over half of its electricity. South Africa's economic success is founded on mineral wealth, including gold, diamonds and coal. It also has the best-developed infrastructure, including transport and communications, of any African nation.

RADICAL CHANGE

South Africa is a major force in both African and world politics. It is now among the most liberal democracies in Africa, with a constitution banning discrimination of any kind. However, until the 1990s South Africa was ruled by one of the world's most repressive regimes. It underwent radical and tumultuous change in the early 1990s. For more than a century, a minority white population of mainly Dutch or English descent ruled this predominantly black nation. Whites owned most of the land and lived a comfortable lifestyle by exploiting South's Africa's mineral riches and its non-white population. The majority black population mainly lived in poverty and could not even vote.

▼ On 27 April 1994, long queues formed all over South Africa as people waited to vote in the country's first-ever democratic election.

World in Focus
South Africa

JEN GREEN

WAYLAND

First published in 2006 by Wayland
© Wayland 2006

Commissioning editor: Nicola Edwards
Editor: Nicola Barber
Inside design: Chris Halls, www.mindseyedesign.co.uk
Cover design: Wayland
Series concept and project management by EASI-Educational Resourcing
(info@easi-er.co.uk)
Statistical research: Anna Bowden
Maps and graphs: Martin Darlison, Encompass Graphics

British Library Cataloguing in Publication Data
Green, Jen
    South Africa. - (World in focus)
    1.South Africa - Juvenile literature
    I.Title
    968'.066

ISBN-10: 0750247444
ISBN-13: 978-0-7502-4744-3

Printed and bound in China

Wayland, 338 Euston Road, London NW1 3BH

Wayland, Hachette Children's Books
Level 17/207 Kent Street
Sydney, NSW 2000

Cover top: Campaigners on a march in the Eastern Cape to mark World AIDS day.
Cover bottom: Tourists on safari in the Kruger National Park.
Title page: Table Mountain rises above Cape Town.

Picture acknowledgements. The author and publisher would like to thank the following for allowing their pictures to be
reproduced in this publication:
Corbis *cover top*, 4, 37, 45 (Gideon Mendel), 5 (Peter Turnley), 6 (Martin Harvey), 9 (Hulton-Deutsch Collection), 10, 11
(Bettmann), 13 (Reuters), 15 (Rob C. Nunnington; Gallo Images), 16 (Wayne Conradie/epa), 20 (Richard T. Nowitz), 21, 32
(Charles O'Rear), 28, 39, 41, 57 (Mike Hutchings/Reuters), 27 (Michael S. Lewis), 29 (Owen Franken), 30 (Caroline Penn),
34 (Wally McNamee), 38 (Jon Hicks), 46 (Anthony Bannister; Gallo Images), 49 (Ed Kashi), 51 (Mike Blake/Reuters), *cover
bottom,* 53 (Louise Gubb), 56 (Sergio Pitamitz), 58 (David Lewis/Reuters); Corbis Saba 12, 23, 31 (Louise Gubb); Corbis
Sygma 25 (Silva Joao), 36 (UN/DPI), 54 (Jon Hrusa/I); EASI-Images *title page* 8, 14, 17, 19, 22, 24, 26 (Tony Binns), 18, 33,
35, 40, 42, 43, 44, 47, 48, 50, 52, 55, 59 (Roy Maconachie).

The website addresses (URLs) included in this book were valid at the time of going to press. However, because of the
nature of the Internet, it is possible that some addresses may have changed, or sites may have changed or closed down
since publication. While the author and Publishers regret any inconvenience this may cause the readers, no responsibility
for any such changes can be accepted by either the author or the Publisher.

The directional arrow portrayed on the map on page 7 provides only an approximation of north.

The data used to produce the graphics and data panels in this title were the latest available at the time of production.

Throughout the 1900s, non-white South Africans waged a tremendous struggle against white rule: first by peaceful means such as demonstrations, and finally by civil disobedience and sabotage. From the 1950s, the white minority, known as Afrikaners, had introduced a system of racial separation to enforce their rule. It was known as *apartheid*, which means 'apartness' in Afrikaans, the Afrikaner language. In the 1960s and '70s the ruling party, the National Party, introduced increasingly repressive laws to maintain white control. South Africa became more and more isolated as countries around the world condemned its racist regime. As apartheid intensified it looked as if the country was heading for bloody revolution. Instead, in around 1990 the National Party finally bowed to both internal and external pressures and began to dismantle apartheid. Within a few short years, the whole system was overturned in a 'negotiated revolution'. The African National Congress (ANC), which had opposed white supremacy since the early 1900s, swept to victory in the country's first democratic election in 1994. Nelson Mandela, jailed for 27 years because of his opposition to apartheid, became the first democratically elected president.

In 1994, Mandela vowed to build a society in which 'all South Africans, both black and white, will be able to walk tall, without any fear in their hearts'. However, the new government faced enormous challenges. Radical political change did not provide an instant levelling-out of the huge inequalities that had arisen under white rule. Since 1994, the government has done much to improve housing, general living standards and educational and job opportunities for non-whites. However deep divisions still exist within South African society in terms of wealth, land, education and employment. About half the country's population still lived in poverty in the early 2000s. Meanwhile new challenges arose, including HIV/AIDS on an epidemic scale (see page 45).

▲ On 11 February 1990, Nelson Mandela addressed a huge crowd of anti-apartheid supporters just hours after his release from prison.

LAND AND PEOPLE

Located at the southern tip of Africa, South Africa shares borders with Namibia, Botswana, Zimbabwe, Mozambique and Swaziland. It completely encloses the land-locked country of Lesotho. Measuring up to about 1,400 km (870 miles) from north to south and 1,600 km (990 miles) from east to west, South Africa is about twice the size of Texas. It is a land of great natural beauty and scenic variety. Much of the country is a high plateau with rolling grasslands, but there are also fertile valleys, craggy peaks and large expanses of scrubland and desert. South Africa's scenic beauty, sweeping beaches and spectacular wildlife form the basis of its thriving tourist industry (see pages 52-3). South Africa has not one but three capitals. Pretoria (Tshwane) in the northeast is the administrative capital, holding many government buildings. Cape Town in the southwest is the legislative capital, the seat of parliament. Bloemfontein in the centre is the judicial capital, location of the Supreme Court.

South Africa is one of the most ethnically diverse countries in Africa. As well as a majority black population made up of Zulu, Xhosa and many other groups, the country also has the largest population of Europeans, Indians, and people of mixed race (also known as Coloureds) of any African nation. It is nicknamed the 'rainbow nation' because of this diversity.

Reflecting its ethnic makeup, the country has eleven official languages: Afrikaans, English, and nine Bantu tongues: isiNdebele, North Sotho, Setswana, Sesotho, siSwati, Shangaan-Xitsonga, isiVenda, isiXhosa and isiZulu. South Africa is second only to India in its total of official languages. Xhosa is known for its 'click' syllables, with 18 different click sounds. Zulu is the most widely spoken language in South Africa, but English is increasingly used to bridge language barriers. Some sections of the population are concerned that English is becoming more dominant, at the expense of certain African languages. As well as these official languages, many other languages and dialects are also spoken.

Physical geography

- 📁 Land area: 1,219,912 sq km/471,008 sq miles
- 📁 Water area: 0 sq km/0 sq miles
- 📁 Total area: 1,219,912 sq km/471,008 sq miles
- 📁 World rank (by area): 25
- 📁 Land boundaries: 4,862 km/3,021 miles
- 📁 Border countries: Botswana, Lesotho, Mozambique, Namibia, Swaziland, Zimbabwe
- 📁 Coastline: 2,798 km/1,739 miles
- 📁 Highest point: Njesuthi (3,408 m/11,181 ft)
- 📁 Lowest point: Atlantic Ocean (0 m/0 ft)

Source: CIA World Factbook

◄ South Africa's beautiful scenery and spectacular wildlife are a major draw for tourists.

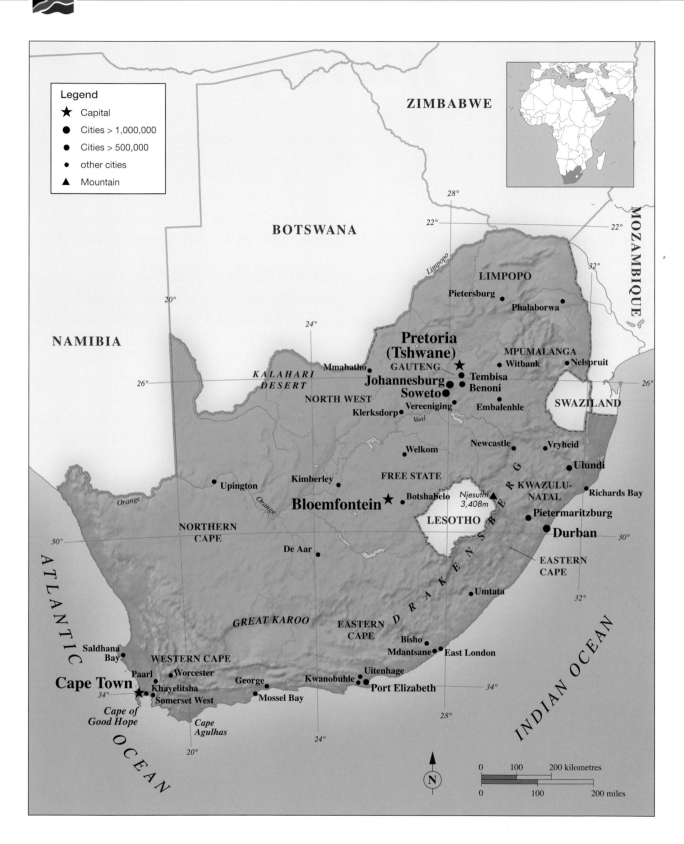

Legend
★ Capital
● Cities > 1,000,000
● Cities > 500,000
• other cities
▲ Mountain

ZIMBABWE

MOZAMBIQUE

BOTSWANA

28°
22°　22°
32°

LIMPOPO
• Pietersburg
• Phalaborwa

NAMIBIA

20°

24°

KALAHARI DESERT

26°

MPUMALANGA
★ **Pretoria (Tshwane)**
GAUTENG
• Mmabatho
• Witbank　• Nelspruit
● **Johannesburg**　• Tembisa
● Soweto　• Benoni
NORTH WEST
• Vereeniging　• Embalenhle　SWAZILAND
• Klerksdorp　*Vaal*
26°

• Welkom
• Newcastle　• Vryheid
• Kimberley　FREE STATE　• Ulundi
• Upington　**Bloemfontein** ★ • Botshabelo　KWAZULU-NATAL
Orange　*Njesuthi 3,408m* ▲　• Richards Bay
Orange　LESOTHO　• Pietermaritzburg
NORTHERN CAPE　● **Durban**
30°　30°

• De Aar

D R A K E N S B E R G

EASTERN CAPE

32°

GREAT KAROO　• Umtata

EASTERN CAPE
• Bisho
• Mdantsane　• East London

ATLANTIC

• Saldhana Bay
WESTERN CAPE
• Paarl　• Worcester　• George　• Uitenhage
Cape Town ★　• Khayelitsha　• Kwanobuhle
34°　• Somerset West　• Mossel Bay　• Port Elizabeth　34°
Cape of Good Hope　*Cape Agulhas*

INDIAN OCEAN

28°

O C E A N

20°　24°

N

0　100　200 kilometres
0　100　200 miles

CHAPTER 2

History

The first inhabitants of South Africa were the San (Bushmen) and Khoekhoen people, who roamed South Africa as hunter-gatherers some 10,000 years ago. By 2,000 years ago the Khoekhoen had become sheep- and cattle-herders living as far south as the Cape. A little later, Bantu-speaking Nguni people moved into the area from further north. These included the ancestors of the Zulu, Xhosa and other groups that make up much of the modern black population. These groups herded cattle, forged iron, and built small settlements. During the 14th and 15th centuries AD, more African peoples moved south into the area, including Sotho, Tswana, Tsonga and Venda. Skilled metal workers and farmers, they built villages, some of which developed into towns.

EUROPEAN SETTLERS

European settlement of South Africa dates to 1652, when a Dutch trading company called the Dutch East India Company built a fortified settlement where Cape Town stands today. This port was used to refuel ships sailing between Europe, India and the Far East. During the late 17th and 18th centuries, white settlement of the Cape expanded as the Dutch seized the lands of the Khoekhoen and Xhosa. Dutch farmers called Boers set up farms mainly worked by slaves brought from Indonesia, Madagascar and India. Meanwhile, a steady stream of new settlers arrived from Europe, including Germans and French Protestants called Huguenots.

In 1806, the British seized Cape Colony from the Dutch during the Napoleonic wars. From the 1830s

◀ This monument in Pretoria commemorates the Great Trek of the 1830s-50s, when thousands of Boers migrated from Cape Colony to avoid British domination.

the Boers, also known as Afrikaners, moved to other parts of South Africa to escape British rule. They moved first to Natal, and then, when this too was seized by the British, further north again, where they set up two republics called the Transvaal and Orange Free State.

The 19th century was a time of conflict, not only between Europeans and Africans, but also among black peoples, as the Zulu, Sotho and Ndebele sought to expand their lands. In the 1860s, the discovery of gold and diamonds in the Boer republics brought new waves of white settlers. Boers and British fought for control of mineral-rich lands during the Boer Wars of 1880-1 and 1899-1902. At the same time, both the Boers and the British continued to seize African lands, putting down black resistance with superior weapons. The last armed black resistance was brutally suppressed in 1906. Meanwhile new laws and taxes forced many black Africans into paid employment for whites.

▼ From the 1870s the British waged a series of wars against the Zulus, Xhosa and other African peoples. This drawing shows British officers returning from a negotiation with the Zulu chief Cetshwayo, during a truce in the 1879 Zulu War.

WHITE RULE AND APARTHEID

In 1902 the Second Boer War ended in victory for the British. Eight years later the British and Boer territories were combined to form the Union of South Africa, in which black Africans had few rights. The 1913 Natives' Land Act legalized the land seizures of the 19th century, setting aside all but 13 per cent of the country for whites, despite the fact that whites made up only a small minority of South Africa's population. The 1923 Native Urban Areas Act required blacks in towns to live in areas separate from whites. The African National Congress (originally the South African Native National Congress) was formed in 1912 to oppose the dawning era of white supremacy, but its eloquent appeals for justice were ignored.

After World War II the Afrikaner extremist National Party took power in South Africa. It set out to enforce white minority rule through a system of racial segregation called apartheid. All South Africans were classified by race, with blacks and whites required to live in separate areas and separated in public places such as buses, trains, schools, doctors' waiting rooms, toilets and beaches. In every case, black South Africans were given inferior resources and facilities to whites. In response, the ANC and allied groups called for non-violent protest against apartheid.

UPRISING

In 1960, a group of unarmed demonstrators gathered to protest against the racist Pass Laws

▼ During the apartheid era blacks and whites had to travel in separate train carriages. These black Africans have occupied a 'whites-only' carriage during a protest in 1952.

SLEGS BLANKES
EUROPEANS ONLY.

(see box) in Sharpeville, Transvaal. The police opened fire on the crowd, killing 69 people and wounding 186 more. The Sharpeville Massacre caused a wave of unrest among the black population. The government banned the ANC and allied organizations. Activists including Nelson Mandela went underground and launched an armed force, *Umkhonto we Sizwe* (MK), the 'Spear of the Nation'. MK began a bombing campaign against physical targets such as government buildings that symbolized white rule. In 1962, many activists were arrested, including Mandela who was sentenced to life imprisonment. With its leaders imprisoned, the ANC went into exile to continue the fight.

? Did you know?

In 1961 *Umkhonto we Sizwe* stated: 'The time comes in the life of any nation when there remain only two choices: submit or fight. That time has now come to South Africa.'

Focus on: The Pass Laws

The 1950 Population Registration Act classified South Africans into four racial groups: blacks, whites, Indians and Coloreds. The classification affected every aspect of people's lives, including where they could live and work, their schooling and their freedom of movement. The 1952 Pass Laws required non-whites to carry an identity card or pass at all times. Blacks had to leave whites-only cities by sunset, except for maids working for white households, who were required to live in separate quarters. Anyone found without a pass could be arrested. In the 1950s, the ANC called for mass action against the Pass Laws. Many people burned their passes and 8,000 people were arrested.

▼ South African police walk among the bodies of unarmed protestors, shot dead during the Sharpeville Massacre in 1960.

LIFE UNDER APARTHEID

The Bantustan Acts of the 1960s and '70s strengthened previous acts that had confined black Africans to reserved areas. The new acts required almost all blacks to live in one of ten *bantustans*, or homelands, or in townships on the outskirts of white cities and industrial areas where they serviced white businesses and homes. Making blacks citizens of the homelands meant that they could be denied rights in South Africa itself. The United Nations and many countries condemned the new laws as a violation of human rights, and began to impose trade sanctions on South Africa.

For generations, black Africans had deliberately been given inferior schooling. In 1976 a new law required them to receive half their lessons in Afrikaans, the language of the white rulers. Thousands of young people protested against this law. When police fired on a demonstration in the township of Soweto near Johannesburg, over 600 people were killed, including many children. Outrage swept the townships. The international community condemned the massacre, and the ANC called for the townships to rise up and become 'ungovernable'.

APARTHEID CRUMBLES

During the 1980s the South African government became ever-more isolated. Supporters of anti-apartheid launched strikes and demonstrations on a massive scale. In 1983, the National Party announced a state of emergency, with new

▼ In 1989 the South African police were still using force to suppress anti-apartheid protests. Here, a police helicopter sprays sand to disperse black demonstrators on a 'whites-only' beach.

powers to put down the growing unrest. Over 3,000 people died and 30,000 were arrested in the following three years, as violence also grew between the ANC and its main rival group Inkatha, a powerful Zulu political party headed by Chief Mangosuthu Buthelezi. Meanwhile trade sanctions were crippling the economy. In addition, South Africa suffered defeat in a series of unofficial wars waged against other African countries opposed to apartheid, notably Angola.

By 1989, the country truly had become 'ungovernable', as the anti-apartheid demonstrators had hoped, and the National Party realized it could no longer maintain white minority rule. A new leader, F.W. de Klerk, was elected president. Within a few months the government announced plans to replace apartheid with a new multi-racial democracy. The ANC was unbanned, political prisoners including Mandela were released, and the apartheid laws repealed. Black leaders began talks with the government to organize

the changeover to majority rule. In 1994 South Africa held its first democratic election. The ANC took power with Nelson Mandela as president. The world's first-ever 'negotiated revolution' had taken place.

Focus on: Nelson Mandela

Nelson Mandela was born in 1918. Trained as a lawyer, he joined the ANC to campaign for black rights. When the ANC was banned in 1960, Mandela went into hiding and helped to found *Umkhonto we Sizwe*. He was soon arrested and tried, along with 155 other activists, and was sentenced to life imprisonment. During the 27 years he spent in jail, Mandela's fame spread worldwide, and he came to symbolize the struggle against apartheid. Released in 1990, he was elected president in 1994. Among other accomplishments, he helped to form the groundbreaking Truth and Reconciliation Commission (see page 25) to help heal the social wounds of apartheid. Mandela stepped down as president in 1999.

◀ In 1993, F.W. de Klerk and Nelson Mandela were jointly awarded the Nobel Peace Prize for their work in bringing about a peaceful end to apartheid.

CHAPTER 3

Landscape and Climate

Occupying 1,219,912 sq km (471,008 sq miles), South Africa is about the size of France and Spain combined. The Atlantic Ocean forms the country's western boundary, with the Indian Ocean to the east. The waters of the two oceans mingle at Cape Agulhas, at Africa's southernmost tip.

GEOGRAPHY AND TERRAIN

Four main types of terrain are found in South Africa: plateauland, mountains, coastal plains and deserts. A high plateau called the Veld, Afrikaans for 'field', covers much of the interior and extends northeast towards Zimbabwe. The Highveld, lying at altitudes ranging from 1,200 m to 1,800 m (3,900-5,900 ft), occupies much of the central area. In the northwest, the Middleveld lies at about 1,200 m (3,900 ft), while in the northeast, the Transvaal Basin is mostly less than 1,000 m (3,280 ft). To the east and south, the Veld is rimmed by a semicircular mountain chain called the Great Escarpment, which includes the craggy peaks of the

▼ The distinctive flat-topped shape of Table Mountain rises above Cape Town.

Drakensberg – Afrikaans for 'Dragon's Mountains'. Another mountain range, the Cape Mountains, rises in the south, while Cape Town is overshadowed by the famous flat-topped Table Mountain. The Great and Little Karoo are two dry plateaus located between the Cape and Drakensberg ranges.

Much of South Africa's coastline is edged by a strip of lowland. The western strip is quite narrow, just 60 km (37 miles) wide, while the eastern strip is more extensive, measuring 80-240 km (50-150 miles) wide. The eastern strip rises steeply to the Great Escarpment. In the northwest, the barren Kalahari Desert stretches into Botswana, while the Namib Desert occupies the western strip.

South Africa has few major rivers because of its mainly dry climate. The longest river, the Orange, runs 2,100 km (1,300 miles) from Lesotho west to the Atlantic Ocean. Other notable rivers include the Vaal, a tributary of the Orange, which is 1,200 km (745 miles) long, and the Limpopo, flowing 1,770 km (1,100 miles) from near Johannesburg to the Indian Ocean in Mozambique. Increasing use of water by agriculture and also cities and industry is depleting South Africa's rivers and groundwater supplies (see page 55).

> ▶ The Orange River has worn a deep gorge where it flows through an area of soft rock in the Augrabies Falls National Park.

Focus on: Natural hazards

Drought is the most serious hazard in South Africa (see page 17). One of the worst droughts of recent years was in 1991-2. Bushfires sometimes start in drought-stricken areas. Tropical storms called cyclones may sweep in off the Indian Ocean in humid weather, damaging settlements on the east coast. Tornadoes may strike either coastal or inland regions in summer. In 1993, a powerful tornado killed seven people in the east of the country in the towns of Glencoe and Utrecht.

CLIMATE

Located about midway between the Equator and the Antarctic, South Africa has a broadly mild, sunny climate with many regional variations. Situated in the southern hemisphere, winter falls between June and August, with summer between December and February. The main influences on regional climates are latitude, height above sea level, prevailing winds, and distance from the ocean. Mountains and plateaus have cooler temperatures than coastal regions. The city of Johannesburg, which lies on a high ridge called the Witwatersrand, has January averages of 18°C (64°F) and July averages of 10°C (50°F). In the highest parts of the Highveld, winter temperatures drop below freezing point at night.

▼ A farmer of the Northern Cape finds his stock dead of thirst during a drought in 2004. Six regions of South Africa were declared disaster zones during this drought, the worst in a century.

The southwest has a Mediterranean climate, with warm, dry summers and cool, wet winters. Cape Town has average January highs of 26°C (79°F) and midwinter lows of 7°C (45°F). In the east, the warm, southward-flowing Mozambique and Agulhas ocean currents give the coastal strip a subtropical climate with hot, humid summers

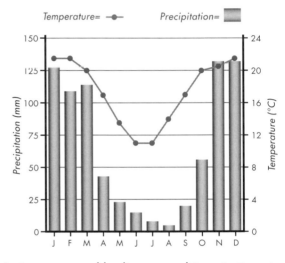

▲ Average monthly climate conditions in Pretoria

and dry, bright winters. The port of Durban on the east coast has average January temperatures of 24°C (75°F) and winter averages of 18°C (64°F). The cold Benguela Current flowing north along the west coast brings cooler temperatures to the western coastal strip.

Rainfall is generally low and unreliable in South Africa, with droughts occurring when the rains fail. Rainfall decreases from east to west, with the east and south being the wettest regions, while the north and west are much drier. The eastern strip is watered by moist winds blowing off the Indian Ocean, with some places receiving 100 cm (39 in) of rain yearly. The Benguela Current lowers temperatures along the west coast, which prevents rain clouds from forming. Desert conditions, with less than 5 cm (2 in) of rain yearly, prevail in parts of the north and west.

? Did you know?

Sixty-five per cent of South Africa receives less than 50 cm (20 in) of rainfall a year.

VEGETATION

Climate, terrain and soil type produce a huge range of vegetation in South Africa. The humid east coast has a subtropical vegetation including yellowwood and ironwood trees and coastal mangroves. The plateauland of the Veld is covered with savannah grasslands scattered with acacia trees, with the more densely wooded Bushveld in the northeast. In the west, dry Namaqualand bursts into a carpet of flowers after winter rains have fallen. The Southwestern Cape is famous for its unique vegetation, known as *fynbos* (fine-leaved bush). Plants here include colourful proteas, ericas, pelargoniums and irises.

? Did you know?

South Africa has a huge variety of plants – over 23,000 species, representing one-tenth of the world's plants.

▼ The king protea, South Africa's national flower, is a spectacular example of *fynbos* vegetation.

CHAPTER 4

Population and Settlements

According to figures compiled in the census of 2001, South Africa's population is made up of 79 per cent blacks, 9.6 per cent whites, 8.9 per cent people of mixed race, and 2.5 per cent Asians. The black population consists of many different groups, each with its own cultural heritage, language and traditions. The largest group, the Nguni, includes Zulu, Xhosa and Swazi. The next-largest, Sotho, includes Sesotho, Bapedi and Tswana. The Shangaan-Tsonga and Venda are also major groups.

Most whites are of European descent, of either Dutch, German, French-Huguenot or British extraction. The term Coloureds, used for people of mixed race, includes the 'Cape Malays', the descendants of Southeast Asians brought to Africa as slaves, and the Khoisan (the collective name for the Khoekhoen and San peoples, the original inhabitants of South Africa; see page 8). The Asian population is mostly Indian, descended from indentured labourers brought to work in the plantations of Natal in the 19th century. Other substantial populations include over 10,000 Chinese people.

POPULATION GROWTH AND DENSITY

In 2005, South Africa had a population of 47.4 million. The population grew rapidly from the 1970s to the 1990s. However from 2000-2005 it grew by just 0.6 per cent per annum. South Africa's population is now forecast to fall slightly, to 42 million by 2030. The major reason for the recent decline in population growth is the high number of people with HIV/AIDS (see

? Did you know?

Only a few San and Khoekhoen remain in South Africa. Small groups of San (Bushmen) live a nomadic life in the Kalahari Desert.

◄ South African society is now better integrated than at any time during the 20th century. These medical students attend the University of Cape Town.

page 45) which has caused the mortality and infant mortality rate to rise since the 1990s. The number of whites who left South Africa either during or following the apartheid years has also affected population figures. In 2003, a little under one-third of the population was under 15, with nearly two-thirds aged between 15 and 64, and only a small percentage over 65.

Although the average population density across the whole of South Africa is 39 people per sq km (100 per sq mile), in practice the population is unevenly distributed. Very few people live in the north and northwest, where the dry climate makes farming difficult or impossible, and where there are few natural resources. The southwestern tip around Cape Town and the

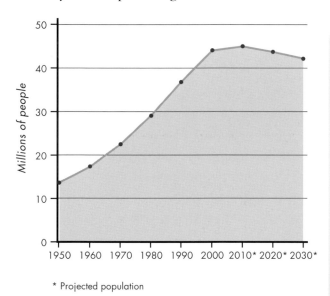

* Projected population

▲ Population growth 1950-2030

Population data

📂 Population: 47.4 million

📂 Population 0-14 yrs: 32%

📂 Population 15-64 yrs: 64%

📂 Population 65+ yrs: 4%

📂 Population growth rate: 0.5%

📂 Population density: 38.9 per sq km/100.6 per sq mile

📂 Urban population: 57%

📂 Major cities: Cape Town 3,103,000 Johannesburg 3,288,000, Durban 2,643,000 Pretoria 1,282,000

Source: United Nations and World Bank

◀ A street market adds colour to Johannesburg's high-rise city centre. This ex-mining community is now the nation's largest city.

eastern coastal strip are both much more densely populated. On the Highveld, Gauteng Province includes the large cities of Johannesburg, Soweto, Pretoria and Vereeniging. The wetter climate of the south and east favours farming, while mining and industry also provide sources of employment.

URBAN AREAS

In 2003, 57 per cent of the population lived in urban areas, including most whites, Asians and people of mixed race. This figure has risen steadily in recent decades. Cape Town, Johannesburg and Durban are the largest cities, with over 2.5 million inhabitants. Soweto, Pretoria, Port Elizabeth and Pietermaritzburg are also major urban centres.

During the 20th century, racial segregation had a major impact on urban development. Sprawling black townships sprang up around whites-only cities to house the workers needed to run mines, factories and service industries. Originally the townships were makeshift shanty settlements. Permanent dwellings were built from the 1940s, but before 1994 most homes in townships lacked electricity or proper sanitation. Townships also had few facilities such as shops, parks, schools or community centres. Since 1994 the government has begun a massive building and modernizing programme (see box), but progress has been slow. Many homes in townships are still without adequate sanitation and power supplies.

During the apartheid era, many township-dwellers travelled long distances each day to work in city centres. In the post-apartheid era, some black families have moved closer to city centres. However in general, urban dwellings still reflect the gulf between rich and poor. Leafy suburbs that were once whites-only districts have luxury homes with swimming pools, and most of these homes remain white-owned.

RURAL AREAS

Around 43 per cent of South Africa's population, predominantly blacks, live in rural areas. Here, too, facilities are often basic, with many homes lacking sanitation and electricity. Traditional dwellings are thatched with straw and often

◀ Most of the houses in the exclusive beach-front neighbourhood of Clifton in Cape Town are still owned by whites.

Focus on: Building new homes

In 1994, the new government inherited the housing crisis of the apartheid era, with up to 3 million families homeless and up to 8 million people living in shanty towns or squatter camps. Its Reconstruction and Development Programme (RDP) included a major building programme, with the challenge of constructing 300,000 new homes before 2004. New estates now cover large areas on the outskirts of cities. However shortage of housing is still a major problem in cities because, despite the government's efforts, the demand for housing in cities has outstripped the provision of new housing. This is largely a result of mass migration into the cities from rural areas. In 2003-4, an estimated 7 million people were still living in shanty towns.

built of mud bricks. Zulu and Xhosa homes are traditionally circular, while Ndebele and Basotho dwellings are rectangular, and decorated with geometric designs in bright colours.

The land acts of the 20th century uprooted millions of black Africans from their homes, transporting them to reserved areas which became the *bantustans* (homelands; see page 12). Small-scale farmers were turned off their lands. During these forced relocations, thousands of people were simply abandoned without housing or employment. During the apartheid era, *bantustan* populations consisted largely of women, children and older people, with men working as migrant labourers in distant mines and factories. Since 1994 the government has faced a massive challenge in trying to right some of the injustices of apartheid, including restoring confiscated lands.

▼ The walls of Ndebele homes are decorated with bold patterns in strong colours, that the women paint by hand.

CHAPTER 5

Government and Politics

South Africa has been a republic since 1961, when it was expelled from the British Commonwealth (see page 34). It is a parliamentary democracy, with a constitution dating from 1996. Since 1994 everyone over the age of 18 has had the right to vote. Before that time, black Africans had no vote.

NATIONAL AND REGIONAL GOVERNMENT

South Africa's parliament is made up of two houses. The upper house, the National Council of Provinces, has 90 members, with ten members elected from each province. The lower house, the National Assembly, has 400 members, with half being drawn from national and half from provincial lists. Members are elected by proportional representation, and elections are held every five years. The president is head of government, and appoints the Cabinet. Unlike many other nations, he or she is also head of state. Thabo Mbeki of the ANC has been president since 1999, when Nelson Mandela stepped down.

The Republic of South Africa incorporates all the former *bantustans* (homelands). It is divided into nine provinces: Limpopo, North West

▼ The South African government is based at parliament buildings in the legislative capital, Cape Town.

Province, Gauteng, Mpumalanga, KwaZulu-Natal, Free State, and the Northern, Western, and Eastern capes. Provincial governments are headed by an elected premier, who appoints an executive council. Both provincial and local councils have considerable independence on issues such as taxation. In addition, a council of traditional leaders advises the government on a national, provincial and local level.

CONTEMPORARY POLITICS

Since 1994, the African National Congress (ANC) has been the most popular party in South Africa, winning 69.7 per cent of the vote in the 2004 election. It currently rules in coalition with the Inkatha Freedom Party (IFP), led by Chief Mangosuthu Buthelezi. Other important political parties include the Democratic Alliance (DA), the African Christian Democratic Party (ACDP), the Pan-Africanist Congress (PAC) and the United Democratic Movement (UDM). In addition both the Communist Party and the Congress of South African Trade Unions (COSATU), active

in the anti-apartheid movement, are formally allied to the ANC. Some sections of the population, notably Zulu-speakers in KwaZulu-Natal, want more autonomy and even independence for certain regions.

Focus on: The Bill of Rights

South Africa's Bill of Rights (which forms part of the 1996 constitution) is among the most liberal and comprehensive in the world. It outlaws discrimination on the grounds of race, religion, gender, language and sexual orientation. All citizens are equal before the law, and guaranteed freedom of opinion, belief and also freedom of movement.

Did you know?

The National Party (the all-white, ruling party of the apartheid era) disbanded in 2005 after failing to win a significant share of the vote in several elections.

◀ Presidential candidate, now president, Thabo Mbeki of the ANC campaigns during the run-up to the 1999 election. The ANC has dominated elections since 1994.

RIGHTING WRONGS

In 1994, the newly-elected government faced immense challenges. The ANC's landslide victory did nothing to change the reality that much of the country's land, wealth and commerce lay in the hands of whites. Most blacks, Coloreds and Asians were less well-educated, with inferior housing and medical services, and higher unemployment. The new government's task amounted to a comprehensive reorganization of society aimed at a fairer distribution of resources. Part of its response was to launch the ambitious Reconstruction and Development Programme (RDP), a 25-year plan to redistribute land, provide jobs and improve housing, medical care and education.

Part of the funding for the RDP came from raising taxes and making cuts in government spending, but much came from private business and foreign aid. By 2004, South Africa had built up foreign debts estimated at US$27 billion.

Since 1994, the government has made great strides in raising living standards for blacks, Coloreds and Asians, but inevitably there are many who feel that progress has been slow. At the other end of the scale, some whites feel that ANC policies have made it difficult for them to find work. Under apartheid, high-paying jobs were reserved strictly for whites. Now whites

▼ Construction workers labour on a building site in Welkom, Free State, in the mid-1990s. This project was one of the many undertaken as part of the Reconstruction and Development Programme of the post-apartheid years.

must compete with everyone else for the first time. The government's Black Economic Empowerment programme (BEE) has proved controversial in its moves to correct racial imbalance in the management of industry and business, where white managers continue to dominate.

As well as the social challenges outlined above, the government also faces a major problem with HIV/AIDS (see page 45) and a very high rate of violent crime, including murder, rape, assault and theft. During apartheid and in the run-up to 1994, many acts of violence were committed by all sides, including the white security forces, the ANC and Inkatha. The Truth and Reconciliation Commission (see box) did much to reduce racial tensions, but many criticize the government's record on law and order, condemning both the police and courts as inept. Since 1994, there have been allegations of corruption within the police force, legal system and even government ministries. In June 2005, vice-president Jacob Zuma was forced to resign after his financial advisor was accused of corruption.

Focus on: The Truth and Reconciliation Commission

◀ No-one was exempt from appearing before the Truth and Reconciliation Commission. Winnie Madikizela-Mandela, former wife of Nelson Mandela, appeared before the commission in 1997 to answer allegations of wrongdoing, such as supporting violence in the last days of apartheid.

The South African government's ground-breaking Truth and Reconciliation Commission was set up in 1995 to heal the wounds of apartheid. Chaired by Archbishop Desmond Tutu, it investigated human rights violations committed between 1960 and 1994. The televised sessions heard statements from thousands of victims and also self-confessed apartheid criminals. It awarded compensation and gave amnesty to those whose crimes were 'politically motivated'. The Commission found the minority white government and also both the ANC and Inkatha guilty of violent acts.

CHAPTER 6

Energy and Resources

South Africa's rich mineral resources include gold, diamonds and abundant coal for energy. Natural resources include arable land, fish in the surrounding seas and also scenic beauty and wildlife, which underpin the tourist industry (see page 52).

ENERGY RESOURCES AND USE

South Africa's energy sector is well developed. It is Africa's leading energy producer and also consumer. Coal is the main source of energy. The country has huge reserves of this fossil fuel – enough to meet its own energy needs and also to make it the world's third-largest coal exporter in the early 2000s. The nation's 60 coal mines provide the raw materials for over 90 per cent of its electricity production. South Africa also has reserves of natural gas, but no oil. However a South African company called Sasol converts coal and gas into synthetic petrol and diesel which are used as fuels. Hydroelectricity is well developed. Dams and hydroelectric plants on the Orange River provide energy and also water for agriculture and nearby cities. Nuclear power contributed 5.4 per cent of the nation's electricity in 2002.

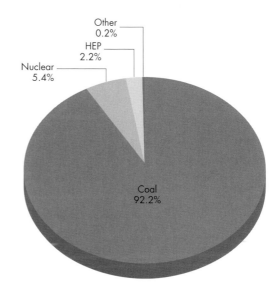

Other 0.2%
HEP 2.2%
Nuclear 5.4%
Coal 92.2%

▲ Electricity production by type

► A hydroelectric dam on the Orange River in Free State. Hydroelectricity provides over 2 per cent of South Africa's electricity.

In 2005, South Africa was ranked 26 in the world in terms of population, yet it used only just over one per cent of the world's energy. In that year, 46 per cent of all energy used in South Africa was consumed by industry, nearly one-quarter by transport, while domestic use accounted for over one-fifth. However, in 1994, around half of the population was without electricity. Part of the 1994 election pledge was to supply electricity to millions of new homes by 2010. Large amounts of money are also being spent on updating the country's dilapadated electricity distribution network, particularly in rural areas.

Energy data

- Energy consumption as % of world total: 1.1%
- Energy consumption by sector (% of total),

Industry:	46.2%
Transportation:	24.4%
Agriculture:	3.1%
Services:	3.7%
Residential:	20.9%
Other:	1.7%

- CO_2 emissions as % of world total: 1.5%
- CO_2 emissions per capita in tonnes p.a.: 8.1

Source: World Resources Institute

MINERAL WEALTH

South Africa's abundant minerals are a major source of income. The discovery of gold and diamonds in the 1860s, '70s and '80s led to its transformation into an industrial nation. The world's top producer of gold, platinum and chromium, South Africa also has rich reserves of manganese, nickel, copper, phosphates, uranium, silver and iron ore.

From the late 19th century, gold and diamonds made vast fortunes for white mine-owners such as Cecil Rhodes of De Beers Consolidated Mines. Meanwhile thousands of non-white miners endured harsh and extremely dangerous conditions for very little pay. During the early 20th century, black and migrant workers were treated little better than slaves, being housed in racially-segregated compounds even before apartheid. Since 1994, the government and mining unions have worked together to improve conditions in the mines.

? Did you know?

In 1905, the world's largest diamond was found near Pretoria. It was cut to form 105 stones, of which the biggest, the Star of Africa, now forms part of the British crown jewels.

◀ A miner working deep underground at a gold mine in Carletonville. Despite modern technology, gold mining is still a dirty and sometimes dangerous occupation.

Focus on: Gold and diamond mining

South Africa's main gold-bearing rocks lie in the Witwatersrand, a 430-km (265-mile) arc between Free State and Mpumalanga. In 1886, a poor prospector named George Harrison discovered gold at what is now Johannesburg. This sparked one of the biggest gold rushes in history. In the space of just three years, the mining town that sprang up became South Africa's largest city. Originally gold was found at the surface, but now gold-bearing rocks lie mainly deep underground. Diamonds were first discovered in South Africa in 1867. Four years later, a rich diamond field was located at Kimberley. The site is now the location of the world's deepest artificial hole.

▲ A South African fisherman tosses his catch ashore at a Cape Town harbour. In 2005, South Africa took part in a major summit on the role of the fishing industry in reducing poverty in Africa.

FISHING, FORESTRY AND FARMING

With around 2,800 km (1,740 miles) of coastline, fishing is an important industry in South Africa. The waters off the west coast are the main fishing grounds. Here the upwelling of cold, mineral-rich water nourishes microscopic plankton which provide food for an abundant and diverse supply of fish. Hake, anchovies, pilchards, mackerel and herring are all commercially important. Fishing is regulated by the government to preserve fish and shellfish stocks.

Only 4 per cent of South Africa is forested. In the 19th century, large tracts of yellowwood and ironwood trees were felled, reducing the nation's already scant timber stocks. However, South Africa currently fulfils most of its own needs for timber and pulp through managed forestry and replanting.

Croplands occupy around 38 per cent of South Africa, but only around one per cent is under permanent cultivation. Irrigation is necessary in many areas. The main crop-growing regions are the south, east and parts of the Veld. Major crops include maize, wheat, sugar cane, potatoes, fruits such as apples, oranges, pineapples, bananas, and also grapes for wine-making. The main grape-growing area is the southern tip of the Western Cape. South Africa ranked among the world's top ten wine-producing nations in the early

▼ Workers harvest grapes at a vineyard in the Western Cape. This region is the centre of the South African wine industry.

2000s. Beef and dairy cattle are pastured on less fertile land, with sheep and goats grazing dry terrain in the north and west, and on the steep slopes of the Drakensberg.

Two main types of farming are practised in South Africa: commercial and subsistence farming. Commercial farms are large-scale enterprises using modern methods and employing mostly black labour. These traditionally white-owned businesses produce food for cities and also sale abroad. Small-scale subsistence farmers, mainly black South Africans, grow food for their families using basic tools such as hoes. Any surplus food they produce is sold at local markets. From colonial times, many Africans were turned off their lands which were then converted to commercial farms and plantations. Since 1994, the government has worked to restore lands to evicted black farmers and to improve resources for subsistence farmers.

CHAPTER 7

Economy and Income

South Africa is Africa's most industrialized nation, producing up to 30 per cent of the continent's entire Gross Domestic Product (GDP). Economic growth is supported by the country's well-developed infrastructure, which allows products to be efficiently transported both within South Africa and to neighbouring countries. In 2003, it achieved economic growth of only 0.8 per cent, but experts have predicted a period of strong growth over the next years.

? Did you know?

In 2004, 30 per cent of South African workers were employed in agriculture.

SOUTH AFRICA'S ECONOMY

Before the arrival of Europeans, most South Africans lived as herders and farmers, forming self-sufficient communities. From the 17th century, the traditional economy was disrupted first by wars waged by whites, and then by the

Focus on: Women workers

South Africa has traditionally been a male-dominated society. During the 19th and 20th centuries, women of all races generally received a less thorough education than men, with illiteracy high among many black women. Even in the late 20th century, women were often paid less than

men for the same work, and suffered discrimination that hindered them from taking senior positions. In 1994, the ANC vowed to build a non-sexist society, working to redress the gender imbalance and fight discrimination in all sectors of employment.

◀ Women workers at a clothing factory in Soweto. In the textile sector, such factories are traditionally staffed by women, who work for low pay.

► Stockbrokers in a brokerage in Johannesburg. The city is a leading centre for banking and finance.

introduction of new laws and taxes. The Hut Tax of the late 19th century required Africans to pay a tax on their homes to the government, which forced many into paid employment for the first time. Men left their villages to seek work in distant mines and factories – the start of the migrant labour system that caused so much hardship. Local farms were left untended, causing widespread poverty.

Industrial development was kick-started by the discovery of gold and diamonds in the late 19th century, and continued in the early 20th century. The economy boomed in the 1950s and '60s, but it was hit in the 1970s and '80s by the international sanctions imposed because of apartheid. The lifting of trade sanctions in the 1990s has helped the economy to recover and sectors such as tourism to boom.

SERVICE INDUSTRIES

Service industries are the most important sector of the South African economy, employing 45 per cent of the workforce and producing 65 per cent of GDP in 2004. This sector includes finance, banking, tourism, transport, education, government and social services. Financial and legal services are well developed, and tourism is a major source of foreign income.

Economic data

☞ Gross National Income (GNI) in US$: 165,326,000,000
☞ World rank by GNI: 30
☞ GNI per capita in US$: 3,630
☞ World rank by GNI per capita: 94
☞ Economic growth: 0.8%
Source: World Bank

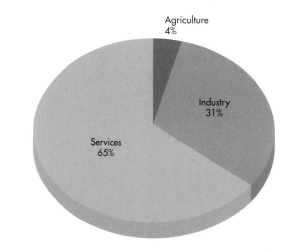

Agriculture
4%

Industry
31%

Services
65%

▲ Contribution by sector to national income.

ECONOMIC MAINSTAYS

Mining and manufacturing are mainstays of the South African economy. In 2004, 25 per cent of the workforce was engaged in this sector, which yielded 31 per cent of GDP. Many manufacturing industries were originally spin-offs from mining. For example, the iron and steel industry grew up to supply mining equipment, while vehicle manufacturing developed to aid the transportation of minerals. South Africa is Africa's main manufacturing nation, and its most important products include vehicles (which contributed 6.4 per cent to GDP in 2003) machinery and electronic equipment, iron and steel, cement, chemicals, fertilizers, textiles, processed foods, gems and jewellery. Johannesburg, Durban, East London and Port Elizabeth are major centres for industry and manufacturing.

WORKFORCE

In 2004, South Africa's workforce was estimated at 16.6 million, with an estimated 26 per cent of the working population unemployed. This unemployment figure includes people working within the informal economy, doing mostly unskilled jobs such as work in the building trade, or selling goods on the streets without being officially registered or paying tax. The government is currently trying to bring more informal-sector workers within the formal economy. Unemployment is particularly high among the black population because of the lack of training opportunities under apartheid. The Reconstruction and Development Programme (see page 24) and other government initiatives have been major sources of employment since 1994.

◀ A worker uses a precision tool to cut a diamond in Jewel City, in Johannesburg.

In 2000, the ANC announced plans to foster economic growth and control inflation by increasing privatization, reducing government spending and relaxing labour legislation. These moves, particularly the last, brought the government into conflict with trade union organizations such as COSATU (see page 23), a traditional ally of the ANC. South Africa's economy is buoyed by foreign investment, which has risen steeply since 1994. However, the economy is still suffering from the legacy of apartheid, which includes widespread poverty and a largely unskilled black workforce (see box). Since 1994 the government has taken steps to tackle these obstacles to economic growth, but they remain daunting problems.

Focus on: A divided workforce

From colonial times through to the apartheid era, South Africa's workforce was divided along racial lines. Whites received better education, training and job opportunities. As a result they secured almost all of the skilled, technical and managerial posts. Non-whites were deliberately less well-educated. They did predominantly manual work and were prevented either by racism or by law from pursuing many professional careers. Since 1994, the government has worked to tackle this imbalance through the Black Economic Empowerment programme and other initiatives. But there is still a great shortage of skilled black workers.

▼ Unemployed women wait in line at an employment office in Cape Town. Unemployment is higher among blacks than whites.

CHAPTER 8

Global Connections

South Africa's ties with other nations include political, economic and cultural connections. Cultural ties have been forged partly through human migration to and from South Africa since colonial times. From the mid-17th century, European settlers began to arrive in increasing numbers. Through slavery or the indentured labour system, they caused the arrival of other immigrants, including slaves from Southeast Asia and eastern and central Africa, and indentured workers from India. Today, people of European, Indian or mixed descent together make up around a fifth of South Africa's population (see page 18).

▼ An anti-apartheid demonstration in Washington DC, the United States, in the 1980s. Similar demonstrations took place in many countries around the world.

INTERNATIONAL RELATIONS DURING APARTHEID

South's Africa's political and economic links with other nations were severely damaged by apartheid. On gaining independence from Britain in 1910, South Africa became part of the British Commonwealth, but it was expelled in the early 1960s because of human rights abuses. Events such as Sharpeville (see page 11) also led to South Africa's expulsion from the Organisation of African Unity (OAU), and from the United Nations (UN) in 1974.

As apartheid intensified, so the country became increasingly isolated. For example, severe restrictions were imposed both on international journalists reporting from South Africa, and on the broadcast of foreign news and media within the country (see page 40). Countries around the

world cut their sporting ties with South Africa, cancelling international events.

During the 1970s and '80s, criticism of apartheid grew internationally. Nelson Mandela became the world's most famous political prisoner, and campaigners in many nations demanded his release. A groundswell of public opinion called for foreign investors to withdraw their backing from South African businesses, and for governments to impose trade sanctions. In 1986, the United States, the European Economic Community (EEC) and the British Commonwealth all imposed trade boycotts on South Africa in response to citizen pressure. The economic boom of the 1950s and '60s had been largely fuelled by foreign investment, so the boycotts were highly damaging. Trade sanctions undoubtedly played a part in forcing the National Party to open negotiations with anti-apartheid groups in 1990.

▲ Tourists at the redeveloped Victoria and Alfred Waterfront in Cape Town. Tourism has boomed in South Africa in the post-apartheid years.

In 1990, Nelson Mandela's release from prison was televised worldwide and watched by millions of people. In 1993, Mandela himself appeared at the UN, requesting that trade sanctions on South Africa be lifted, since the movement toward democracy had become unstoppable. Boycotts were duly lifted, and imports and exports began flowing again. Mandela's inauguration as president of the newly democratic South Africa was witnessed by the largest-ever gathering of international leaders. Sporting links were restored, and tourism quickly became a growth industry. The largely peaceful transition to democracy was a source of inspiration to human rights campaigners around the world.

POST-APARTHEID SOUTH AFRICA

In 1994, South Africa was welcomed back to the Organisation of African Unity (now the African Union, or AU). Since democratization South Africa has been involved in a number of peace talks between African nations, for example, in Ivory Coast, Burundi and the Democratic Republic of the Congo. However, not all aspects of South Africa's foreign policy are popular at home. The government has been widely criticized for its support of the repressive regime in neighbouring Zimbabwe, led by Robert Mugabe. South Africa is also currently engaged in several border disputes (see box).

CURRENT TRADE LINKS AND PARTNERS

South Africa's trading links have blossomed in the post-apartheid era. In 2004, the total value of the country's exports was US$41.9 billion. Its main trading partners were the United States (10.2 per cent of exports), the UK (9.2 per cent), Japan (9.2 per cent), Germany (7.1 per cent) and

> **? Did you know?**
>
> South Africa receives millions of dollars in foreign aid each year: in 2000, the figure was US$487.5 million.

Focus on: Border disputes

Not all of South Africa's relations with its neighbours are peaceful. It has long-standing border disputes with both Swaziland and Namibia. The dispute with Swaziland dates back to the early 1900s, when Swaziland came under British rule. Some areas where Swazi people live have since become part of South Africa, and Swaziland would like the return of these areas.

South Africa's dispute with Namibia is about the exact location of the border between the two countries, and South Africa has troops positioned on the Orange River along this boundary. It also has troops along its border with Zimbabwe, to stem the flow of refugees from that country who are either seeking work or fleeing political persecution.

◀ Nelson Mandela meets with Kofi Annan, Secretary-General of the United Nations, during an Organisation of African Unity summit in 1997.

the Netherlands (4 per cent). South Africa's chief exports include gold, diamonds, platinum and other metals and minerals, coal, machinery, weapons and also foods.

In 2004, South Africa imported goods worth a total of US$39.4 billion. South Africa's main imports are machinery and equipment, chemicals, petroleum products, scientific instruments and foods. South Africa now plays an active role in many political and trade organizations, including the World Trade Organisation, which promotes trade between member states, and the African, Caribbean and Pacific Group of States (ACP). Links with other African nations are also increasing through the South African Development Community (SADC), which coordinates strategies for sustainable development in the region in areas such as trade and industry, food and agriculture, and infrastructure.

► Peaches are among the soft fruit grown for the export market. During the apartheid era, export sales were badly hit by international trade boycotts.

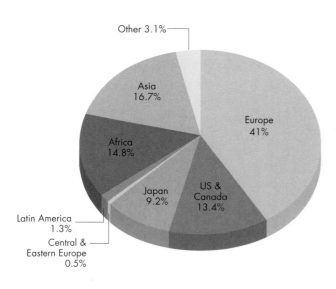

▲ Destination of exports by major trading region

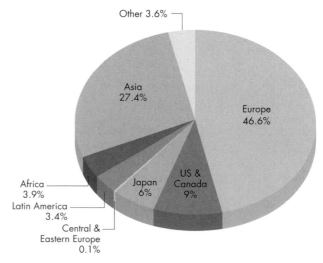

▲ Origin of imports by major trading region

CHAPTER 9

Transport and Communications

South Africa's transport network is well-developed. Ranked as the most efficient in Africa, it is also used by neighbouring nations such as Namibia, Lesotho and Mozambique. The transport sector is a major employer.

RAIL AND ROAD

South Africa's extensive rail network was developed in colonial times to exploit the country's minerals. In 2004, it consisted of some 20,872 km (12,970 miles) of track, of which

Focus on: Gandhi and the railways

The Indian leader Mahatma Gandhi spent over 20 years in South Africa (from 1893 to 1914), working as a lawyer. Although this was well before the apartheid era, discrimination by race was part of everyday life in South Africa. Gandhi's experience of racism on South African trains, and elsewhere, was important to the development of his ideas on non-violent protest. For example, in 1893 Gandhi was ordered to leave a first-class train compartment, despite having a valid first-class ticket, because only whites could use first class. Non-violent protest resulted in his being thrown off the train. After spending years fighting racism in South Africa, Gandhi returned to India, where his technique of passive resistance helped to free the country from British rule. Gandhi's strategy also inspired Dr Martin Luther King, the civil rights leader in the United States.

▼ A steam train crosses the bridge at Dolphin Point, near Wilderness, on the scenic southern 'Garden Route'.

roughly half was electrified. Diesel and electric trains carry freight and millions of commuters daily. There are also steam trains, which are popular with tourists. During the apartheid era, there were separate carriages for whites and non-whites. Experience of segregation on South African trains helped the Indian politician Mahatma Gandhi formulate his opposition to white rule (see box).

In the early 2000s, South Africa had 275,971 km (171,485 miles) of roads, of which less than one-fifth was paved. The country's roads were paved in places where they served (originally white-owned) businesses, while roads in rural areas were largely left unpaved. However, expressways link all major towns and cities and huge amounts of freight go by road. In 2002, fewer than one in ten South Africans owned a car. Most people use public transport including buses to go to work and make other journeys. There are three main kinds of buses: air-conditioned coaches for luxury travel, more ramshackle 'African buses', and cheap minibus taxis, many of which operate illegally.

? Did you know?

During the apartheid years, the United States banned South Africa's national airline from using its airports, in response to pressure from US citizens.

Transport & communications data

- Total roads: 275,971 km/171,485 miles
- Total paved roads: 57,568 km/35,772 miles
- Total unpaved roads: 218,403 km/135,713 miles
- Total railways: 20,872 km/12,970 miles
- Airports: 728
- Cars per 1,000 people: 94
- Mobile phones per 1,000 people: 364
- Personal computers per 1,000 people: 73
- Internet users per 1,000 people: 68

Source: World Bank and CIA World Factbook

◄ A minibus station in Cape Town. Minibuses provide a cheap form of transport and are particularly popular among township-dwellers.

AIR AND SEA

South Africa has three international airports: Johannesburg, Cape Town and Durban. Daily flights link these major hubs with domestic airports at Pretoria, East London, George, Bloemfontein, Kimberley and Port Elizabeth, which in turn are connected to smaller airports. Air travel is an important part of the infrastructure – for those who can afford it. South Africa's sea ports are among the busiest in Africa. The main ports are Cape Town, Durban, East London, Mossel Bay, Port Elizabeth, Richards Bay and Saldhana. Shallows prevent navigation by large vessels of the country's rivers.

PUBLIC TRANSPORT

During apartheid, the Pass Laws required all non-whites to leave the cities where they worked at sunset to return to the townships or suburbs. This placed an enormous strain on public transport – and also on people's pockets,

▼ A bulk cargo vessel takes on grain at Durban. This is South Africa's busiest port, with extensive docks lining the shore.

since commuting was expensive. Millions still have to make long daily journeys from the townships to city centres. Public transport remains overcrowded, costly, and sometimes dangerous because of the risk of mugging. The government has pledged action to ease these problems and new schemes such as a rapid bus transit link in the Cape Town area are currently under construction.

MEDIA AND COMMUNICATIONS

South Africa's media and communications systems are the most modern in Africa. However, during apartheid the media was stifled. Criticism of the government was not permitted, and books, articles, films or plays that presented apartheid in a negative way were banned. For much of the apartheid era, TV was not allowed because multi-racial programmes were common viewing abroad. There were only three radio stations, which were strictly censored. The government took great pains to isolate South Africa so that segregation would seem normal.

South Africa's new constitution guarantees the freedom of the press. Newspapers, TV and other media are now regularly critical of the government. Indeed, suggestions of corruption published in the media have led to the downfall of several prominent politicians, including Winnie Madikizela-Mandela, the divorced wife of Nelson Mandela. The state-run South African Broadcasting Company (SABC) is the main broadcaster. There is also a TV subscription channel and numerous satellite channels. The SABC broadcasts on both TV and radio in English, Afrikaans and many Bantu languages. Over 350 radio stations now operate. Of numerous daily newspapers published in various languages, *The Sowetan* is the top seller in English.

Telecommunications are well developed within large cities, but much less developed in country areas. In 2002, South Africa had 4.8 million land-line phones, with an estimated 16.8 million mobile phones in 2003. Mobile phone use has risen steeply since 1997. In 2002 less than one-twelfth of the population had personal computers, and use of the Internet was also limited, with 3.1 million users. In rural areas and townships, there is often little access to computers, the Internet or a telephone. Telecentres such as Soweto Digital Village are being set up to ease these problems, with mobile centres providing training in computer use.

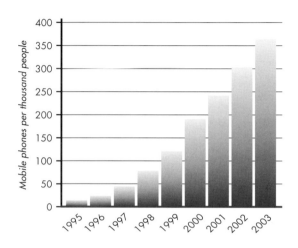

▲ Mobile phone use, 1995-2003

? Did you know?

In 2005, South Africa ranked 26 out of 167 countries in terms of press freedom. This ranking put it ahead of the UK, Australia and Japan.

◄ A customer at a Cape Town barber's shop uses a mobile phone. These phones have eased communication difficulties in some parts of South Africa, although network coverage remains patchy.

CHAPTER 10

Education and Health

In 2002, South Africa spent 8.7 per cent of its Gross Domestic Product on health, and 5.3 per cent on education. The education percentage is one of the highest of any nation, and it looks set to rise to over 8 per cent by 2008.

EDUCATION

During the apartheid era, South Africa's education system was strongly biased towards whites. Large sums were spent on the education of white children, while non-white schools had scant resources. Non-white parents struggled to meet the costs of tuition, uniforms and books. Under apartheid, class sizes of 50 or more were common in black schools, while many white classes had about 20 pupils. Many non-whites failed to complete their schooling, particularly during the period of uprising from 1976 to 1990.

Racism also affected higher education. Of 16 universities in the 1970s and '80s, 11 were for whites only, three for black students, and one each for Asians and people of mixed race. The consequence of this discrimination was a much higher literacy rate among whites than non-whites. A survey of the early 1990s found that almost all white adults were literate, but only 85 per cent of Asians, 75 per cent of Coloreds and 50 per cent of blacks. Since 1994, the government has spent large sums tackling these problems, with significant success. In 2003, 86 per cent of South Africa's population was literate.

The government now aims to provide ten years of education for all children, regardless of race, language or gender. All schools charge fees, but low-income families qualify for fee exemptions. School is compulsory between the ages of seven and 15 (grades 1-9). Children under seven may attend nursery school. Children attend primary school for grades 1 to 7, and move to high school for grades 8 to 9. After grade 9, children may continue with their education for another three years, to grade 12, but this is not compulsory. In the early 2000s, around 90 per cent of all children enrolled at primary school,

◀ A maths lesson in progress at a primary school in Cape Town. Class sizes in mainly black schools are becoming smaller, thanks to the government's commitment to provide equal educational opportunities for all.

but only about 50 per cent of pupils completed their secondary education.

South Africa's 21 universities and 15 *technikons* or technical colleges are open to all students with the required grades. Over 1 million students now attend higher education institutions every year. In 2004, South Africa began to reform its higher education system, with smaller institutions becoming part of larger ones, and technical colleges redefined as universities. As well as education for young people, the government also prioritizes adult education, to address the lack of schooling among those whose education was restricted by the apartheid laws and disrupted by the anti-apartheid struggle. The government's Adult Basic Education and Training (ABET) programme provides secondary-level schooling particularly for the so-called 'lost generation', who missed out on school.

Education and health

- Life expectancy at birth male: 45
- Life expectancy at birth female: 46.5
- Infant mortality rate per 1,000: 53
- Under five mortality rate per 1,000: 66
- Physicians per 1,000 people: 0.7
- Health expenditure as % of GDP: 8.7%
- Education expenditure as % of GDP: 5.3%
- Primary net enrolment: 90%
- Pupil-teacher ratio, primary: 35.4
- Adult literacy as % age 15+: 86%

Source: United Nations Agencies and World Bank

Focus on: Language and schooling

The language in which lessons are taught is a crucial issue in South Africa. In 1976, the ruling that Afrikaans instead of English be taught to black students led to the uprising in Soweto – a major milestone in the struggle against apartheid (see page 12). Primary students now learn in their own languages, but English and Afrikaans are still used at higher levels. Many people feel that African languages are being sidelined by the government's education policy, which fails to challenge English as the dominant tongue.

◄ South Africa's higher education institutions are now multiracial, as this scene in a dining hall at the University of the Western Cape shows. Courses are open to all students who obtain the required grades.

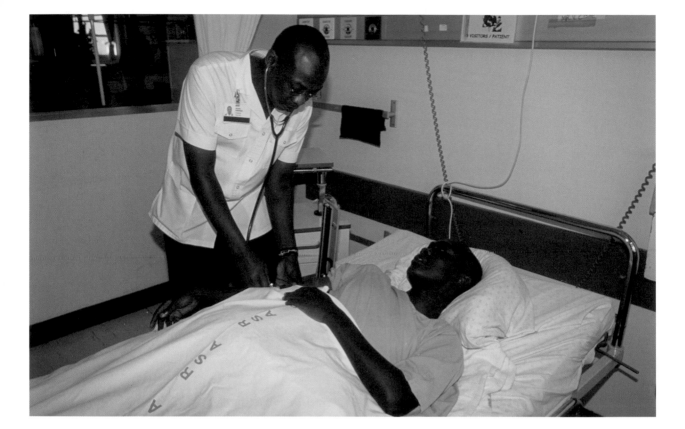

▲ Examining a patient at the Groote Schuur Hospital in Cape Town, where the world's first heart transplant was performed. However, such excellence in medical care is not enjoyed by all South Africans.

HEALTH

In the early 1990s, the average life expectancy for white people was 10 years higher than that for blacks, Coloreds and Asians. This was another legacy of apartheid, during which far more money was spent on medical facilities for whites than for everyone else. Whites who could afford to pay received excellent care, while in non-white settlements, medical centres were scarce and underfunded. In townships and rural areas, poor housing, malnutrition and lack of clean water and sanitation caused diseases such as tuberculosis, cholera, malaria and bilharzia (a worm infection spread through infected water) to be widespread.

In 1994, up to 12 million South Africans were without access to clean drinking water, with up to 20 million without proper sanitation, and 2.3 million malnourished. The ANC vowed to work towards providing all South Africans with equal access to medical care – a challenge of immense proportions. The government commissioned new hospitals and clinics and prioritized training of medical staff. It placed particular importance on ending malnutrition. Pregnant women and children were given free medical care. These policies have brought some improvements in health, but in 2004, there was still less than one doctor (0.7) for every 1,000 people (compared to 1.7 per 1,000 in the UK and 5.5 per 1,000 in the United States). In 2002, 5.9 million people remained without access to a safe source of drinking water, and 14.9 million people still did not have adequate sanitation.

At the start of the 21st century, a huge variety of medical practices coexist in South Africa. Along with orthodox medicine, there are faith healers, herbalists and healers who practise divination (using natural signs to diagnose the cause of illness). Practitioners of all kinds are recognized by the new regime, and are engaged in the effort to raise awareness of health issues.

? Did you know?

In 2004, 27.9 per cent of pregnant women in South Africa were HIV-positive.

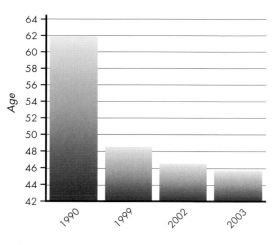

▲ Life expectancy at birth 1990-2003

Focus on: HIV/AIDS

Since 1994, a major health crisis has arisen – HIV/AIDS. In 2004, 21.5 per cent of the adult population in South Africa had HIV/AIDS, and 5.3 million adults and children were infected with HIV – the highest figure of any country in the world. The ANC has been widely criticized for its slowness in reacting to the epidemic, at first failing to acknowledge the extent of the problem and to devote adequate funds to tackling it. As a result, HIV spread quickly. Large sums have now been committed to fight the disease. The high incidence of HIV/AIDS accounts for the steep fall in the average life expectancy in South Africa since 1990 (see graph). Studies in 2004 suggested that the infection rate may soon start to level off, with the number of deaths peaking in 2008.

◀ Campaigners wear HIV-positive T-shirts to challenge prejudice about HIV/AIDS on a march in the Eastern Cape to mark World AIDS day.

CHAPTER 11

Culture and Religion

The ethnic mix of South Africa's 'rainbow nation' has given rise to a rich and varied culture in terms of the arts, cuisine (see box) and religious beliefs. The roots of black South African culture are thousands of years old. From the 17th century onwards, Europeans, Asians and other groups arrived with their own styles and cultures, some of which blended with older traditions to create new forms.

ART AND LITERATURE

South Africa has a rich artistic heritage dating back to prehistoric times. The earliest artists were the San Bushmen, whose rock paintings and carvings can be seen at hundreds of sites today. Mural-painting, mask- and jewellery-making, wood- and stone-carving, basket-weaving and beadwork are among traditional crafts. From the 1650s, Europeans, Asians and other immigrants brought new styles of painting and sculpture. In the mid-20th century, township art became important. Artists such as George Pemba and Mslaba Dumile depicted the harsh realities of township life in their work. Since 1994, the post-apartheid era has brought a new flowering of arts and crafts.

South Africa has a rich literary heritage in English, Afrikaans and the Bantu languages. However, until relatively recently, the black literary tradition was mainly oral. Fables, proverbs and poetry including *izibongo*, praise

▼ A ranger shows San Bushmen rock paintings to visitors in the Kruger National Park.

poems, were handed down by being recited aloud. Olive Schreiner's *Story of an African Farm* (1883) and Percy FitzPatrick's *Jock of the Bushveld* (1907) were early stories in English depicting Afrikaner life.

The anti-apartheid movement gave rise to important literary works including novels, plays and poetry, by both white and non-white writers. Novels such as Alan Paton's *Cry the Beloved Country* (1948) and André Brink's *A Dry White Season* (1979) were banned in South Africa because they challenged the establishment. Nevertheless, they helped to draw the world's attention to the injustices of minority rule. J.M. Coetzee is the only novelist to have won the British Booker Prize twice, while Nadine Gordimer was awarded the Nobel Prize for Literature in 1991. The works of Wilbur Smith and Bessie Head, and Nelson Mandela's autobiography, *Long Walk to Freedom* (1994), are international bestsellers.

? Did you know?

Insect foods such as fried locusts and *mopani* worms are a traditional source of protein in South Africa.

Focus on: South African cuisine

South African cuisine is a varied mix of cooking from different cultures. Dutch, German, Huguenot, Indian, Malay and Chinese immigrants have all contributed distinctive flavours and cooking styles. For example, Cape Malay cuisine features mild meat curries flavoured with spiced fruits. Indian cooking is also hot and spicy. Most European dishes are meat- or fish-based. *Potjiekos*, a stew cooked in a three-legged pot, is a popular recipe. Dried meat, called *biltong*, is chewy but nourishing. Perhaps the most characteristic form of cooking is the *braai* or outdoor barbecue. Barbecued chops, kebabs and *boerewors*, spicy sausages, are served with salads and washed down with local wine or beer. In contrast to these high-protein meals, the diet of many poorer Africans is very simple. The staple food is maize, called mealie, made into a porridge called pap, or used to make meat or vegetable stew.

◄ A craftswoman makes beadwork in a Cape Town workshop. Beadwork produced by projects such as this is sold internationally, including to large stores in London, New York, Paris and Tokyo.

PERFORMING ARTS

Music and dance have always been central to celebrations in South Africa, as well as being part of everyday life. An amazing range of musical styles can be heard, from classical to Cape Malay, jazz, soul, reggae and pop. Black, Asian and Colored musicians bring their own distinctive sounds to western styles from rock to rap. *Kwela* music features the plaintive sound of the penny whistle. *Kwaito* is a fairly new style from the townships, influenced by *toyi-toyi* – protest chants.

During the apartheid years, jazz musicians such as Abdullah Ibrahim, Hugh Masekela, Miriam Makeba and Jonas Gwangwa left South Africa to become internationally famous. Makeba was exiled from South Africa in 1960 because of her appearance in the anti-apartheid movie *Come Back Africa*. Both Makeba and Masekela sang, among other things, about the hardships of apartheid and the need to overthrow it. In the post-apartheid era many musicians have returned home. South Africa has a rich choral tradition including gospel music and Zulu *mbube* (unaccompanied choir singing). Ladysmith Black Mambazo, who joined forces for a time with US singer-songwriter Paul Simon, is one of the best-known choral groups.

RELIGION

South Africa's diverse people follow many different faiths. Over 8 per cent follow traditional African religions, which recognize the influence of ancestral spirits. Spirit mediums called *sangoma* make the connection between ordinary people and the spirit world.

▼ A group of *a capella* or unaccompanied singers produces multi-part harmonies to entertain visitors at the Victoria and Alfred Waterfront in Cape Town.

Over 80 per cent of South Africans are Christians of different denominations. Most Afrikaans-speakers belong to the Dutch Reformed Church. English-speakers include Anglicans, Roman Catholics, Presbyterians and Methodists. Christianity gained hold among black communities in the early 1800s, as black Africans fled the advance of powerful Zulu armies under the Zulu chief Shaka, during a series of wars called the *mfecane* or 'crushing'. Thousands of black Africans sought refuge in Christian missions and were subsequently converted. African independent churches such as the Zion Christian Church blend Christian and traditional beliefs. There are also significant numbers of Muslims and Hindus. Each religion has its own festivals. Christian festivals such as Christmas and Good Friday are public holidays, along with days that celebrate South African history, such as Freedom Day, commemorating the first democratic election on 27 April 1994.

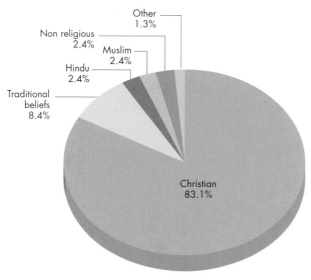

▲ South Africa's major religions

? Did you know?

South Africa's public holidays include Human Rights Day (21 March), the Day of Reconciliation (16 December) and the Day of Goodwill (26 December).

▼ Members of the Church of Zion, which has a mainly Zulu congregation, conduct a baptism in the sea near Durban.

CHAPTER 12

Leisure and Tourism

In the early 2000s, differences in income and living standards among South Africans affected leisure patterns. People living in poverty may have little opportunity for leisure, working long hours to feed their families and taking little time off. During the apartheid years, the migrant labour system split families for months, often years, with men working in distant industries having little leisure time or chance to see their families. Whites-only cities and suburbs were well-supplied with facilities such as parks, sports and community centres, swimming pools, cinemas, cafés, bars and clubs, while in townships and rural areas, these facilities were sparse or non-existent.

Since 1994, the government has worked to improve leisure facilities for blacks, Coloureds and Asians, both in cities and in the countryside. Increased prosperity among some of these groups has meant that more people are able to take time off and get away at least once a year, whether to meet up with distant relatives, go to a beach or national park, or see more of their country. In 2002, nearly 3.8 million South Africans took holidays abroad.

South Africa's sunny climate allows people to spend a lot of free time outdoors. All over the country, children gather on open ground to play soccer, cricket, traditional ball games or tag, known as *kho-kho*. Board games such as

▼ Boys play football on waste ground in Cape Town. Football is one of the sports enjoyed by all South Africans – regardless of colour.

chequers or the traditional game of *morabaraba*, played with tokens called 'cows', are very popular. Elaborate toys such as model cars are made from odds and ends such as wire. South Africans are also keen TV-viewers and movie-goers, with TVs and radios treasured possessions in many households. Township-dwellers who don't possess these items may catch the latest gossip or a TV programme at a local bar, called a *shebeen*.

SPORT

South Africa has a proud sporting tradition, but for much of the 20th century, white people had far better sports facilities than everyone else. Non-whites were often excluded from playing in national teams. As criticism of apartheid grew abroad, South African teams were barred from international competitions, including the Olympic Games. The ban was

lifted in the early 1990s. The South African Sports Commission is working to improve sports facilities and opportunities for everyone. Traditional games and sports such as stick-fighting (with two sticks, one to strike and the other to parry) and *dibeke*, a ball game, are actively encouraged.

Soccer is the most popular sport among all sections of the community. Over 15,000 clubs compete at various levels, and there is a huge following for national and major league teams. Rugby Union is also popular, especially among Afrikaners. There was general delight in 1995 when South Africa hosted and won the Rugby

▼ Swimmers from the South African 4 x 100 metre freestyle relay team celebrate victory at the 2004 Olympic Games in Athens. Swimming is among the sports still dominated at the top level by whites.

World Cup. However, rugby is still dominated by whites at national level, despite efforts to promote the game among blacks, Coloureds and Asians. Cricket, boxing, netball, athletics, tennis and horseracing are also popular. Golf has produced some well-known names, such as Gary Player and Ernie Els. Many people keep fit by cycling, jogging or swimming. The Comrades Marathon (87.6 km between Durban and Pietermaritzburg) and the Two Oceans Marathon (56 km on the Cape peninsula) are two long, gruelling ultra-marathons.

TOURISM

The tourist industry has grown rapidly since apartheid ended. In 1986, just 300,000 tourists visited South Africa. Tourist figures increased dramatically after democratization, and have continued to climb steadily, to 6.5 million in 2003 – a tenfold increase in ten years. With tourism a major source of foreign income, the government promotes the industry, for example regulating

and grading accommodation, and supporting new initiatives such as township tours. Around 10 per cent of the workforce is employed within the tourist industry, whether running hotels, shops or restaurants, working as guides, wardens or drivers, or making handicrafts.

South Africa's spectacular scenery and wildlife are major attractions. Tourists may drive the 'garden route', a scenic stretch of coastline between Cape Town and Port Elizabeth, view the unique *fynbos* vegetation of the Western Cape, head for the beaches around Durban, or hike, bike or climb in the Drakensberg. National parks such as the Kruger are major draws (see box). Visitors may take a safari-style

▼ During the apartheid era, political prisoners including Nelson Mandela were held on Robben Island off Cape Town. The island is now a popular tourist attraction. Here, a guide who was himself once a prisoner shows visitors round.

holiday, go bungee-jumping or white-water-rafting, or explore the traditional cultures of peoples such as the Zulu and Ndebele. The townships have tapped into the tourist trade, with township tours providing income for poor communities. However, security can be an issue for tourists, with high rates of both car theft and mugging.

Tourism in South Africa

- Tourist arrivals, millions: 6.505
- Earnings from tourism in US$: 5,232,000,000
- Tourism as % foreign earnings: 11.5%
- Tourist departures, millions: 3.794
- Expenditure on tourism in US$: 3,232,000,000

Source: World Bank

> **?** ***Did you know?***
>
> Robben Island off Cape Town, where Nelson Mandela spent much of his imprisonment, is now a UNESCO World Heritage Site.

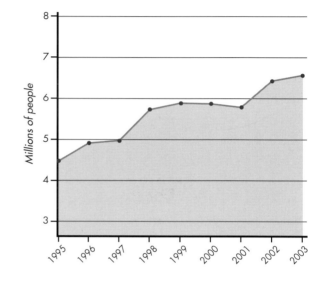

▲ Changes in international tourism, 1995-2003

Focus on: Kruger National Park

Situated on the border with Mozambique, the Kruger National Park is South Africa's largest national park. Covering 19,633 sq km (7,580 sq miles), an area the size of Israel, the reserve dates back to 1898. Visitors may stay in a variety of accommodation, including tents, lodges, and *rondavels* (thatched round houses). People drive or take a safari bus to view zebra, giraffe, antelope and the 'big five': lion, rhino, leopard, elephant and buffalo.

▲ Tourists in the Kruger National Park travel in vehicles like this to view potentially dangerous wildlife, such as these rhinos, in safety.

CHAPTER 13

Environment and Conservation

South Africa's wildlife and vegetation are among the most diverse of any nation. Protection of the natural world lies in the care of the government's Ministry of Environmental Affairs, which has taken a leading role since 1994. The new constitution guarantees the 'environmental rights' of all citizens – the right to a healthy environment, both now and for future generations. The government claims significant success in conserving energy,

▼ In August 2000, environmentalists launched a major conservation effort to clean and move jackass penguins away from an oil slick that threatened their breeding grounds on Dassen Island, near Cape Town.

preventing erosion and reducing air, marine and noise pollution. However environmental needs sometimes conflict with government pledges, for example to improve the standard of housing, and the provision of water and sanitation to townships and shanty towns, and some rural areas.

POLLUTION AND WASTE MANAGEMENT

Mining, industry, agriculture and growing cities all cause problems for the environment. Mining practices pollute the land, with giant spoil heaps littering the skyline around cities such as Johannesburg. Dredging for diamonds and

other minerals also harms marine and wetland environments. Recently the government has halted plans to mine the dunes on the shores of Lake St Lucia near Richards Bay because of the environmental damage that would have resulted. However, in this instance jobs that may be lost due to the prevention of mining could be compensated for by the expansion in tourism around the lake. Mining and overgrazing by livestock also cause erosion and desertification – the expansion of 'dustbowl' areas. Similar problems can arise when forests are felled or natural grasslands ploughed up.

Many of South Africa's rivers, wetlands and coastal waters are polluted in varying degrees by pesticides and fertilizers from agriculture. Lack of water is a general problem because of frequent droughts, and water sources are also being depleted by increasing demands from farms, factories and cities. The government's water conservation agency has launched a major campaign, 'Working for Water', to preserve scant supplies, for example, by clearing non-native plants and trees from water courses and catchment areas. Accidental spills of toxic

▲ A pall of smog hangs in the air over Cape Town. Many South African cities are plagued by this poisonous haze.

chemicals such as oil periodically pollute coastal waters, endangering marine life. Such spills involve expensive clean-up operations. South Africa has signed up to several international treaties that restrict the dumping of waste at sea, including the Law of the Sea, and Ship Pollution treaty.

Air pollution is a problem especially in industrial and urban areas. Waste gases from factories and car exhausts create health concerns such as breathing problems. Sulphur dioxide and nitrogen oxide from cars, power stations and factories give rise to acid rain, which harms land and wetland life. South Africa has signed several treaties to protect air quality, including the Climate Change, Kyoto Protocol, and Ozone Protection treaties. The ANC actively encourages the reuse of resources such as timber, and the recycling of glass, metal, paper and other materials, to curb pollution and also reduce the problem of waste disposal.

HABITAT LOSS AND CONSERVATION

South Africa's wildlife includes many plants and animals found nowhere else. An amazing 80 per cent of its plants, 30 per cent of its reptiles, 15 per cent of its mammals and 6 per cent of its breeding birds are unique. Before the arrival of Europeans, vast herds of grazers such as springbok, wildebeest and zebra roamed the veld. During the 18th and early 19th century, white hunters decimated these herds for meat, sport and to clear the land for domestic stock. The once-prolific bluebuck, the Cape lion and the quagga, a subspecies of zebra, were all hunted to extinction.

Fortunately, the conservation movement became active early, with organizations such as the Wildlife and Environmental Society of South Africa which was founded in 1926. Campaign groups put pressure on governments to set aside wilderness areas. The conservation movement gathered pace in the 1930s. Hunting is now confined to private game reserves where animals are specifically raised for this purpose.

Habitat loss poses a serious threat to wildlife. Expanding cities, industrial areas and farms encroach on wild areas. For example, on the Cape Flats outside Cape Town, sprawling suburbs, factory land and small farms have swallowed up huge tracts of wild grassland and wetland. The government has pledged to protect the nation's wildlife and scenic beauty both for their own sake and to safeguard the lucrative tourist industry. South Africa now has over 500 protected sites including 20 national parks and numerous reserves, marine sanctuaries and botanical

Focus on: Biodiversity

South Africa has been called the 'greatest wildlife show on earth'. Among its 247 species of mammal are the world's largest land animal – the African elephant, the fastest mammal – the cheetah, and the tallest – the giraffe. Over 300 species of breeding birds include colourful bee-eaters and two flightless birds: the jackass penguin and the ostrich, the world's largest bird. Reptiles include crocodiles, sea turtles, and snakes, some of which are highly poisonous.

▶ South African game reserves are regularly patrolled by wardens to protect wildlife such as rhinos and elephants from poachers, who would kill the animals for their horns and tusks.

gardens. Several new national parks have been designated since 1994, including Table Mountain. In 2003, 6.2 per cent of the nation's land area was protected. Whilst representing a huge area, this figure falls short of the 10 per cent recommended for all countries by the International Union for the Conservation of Nature (IUCN).

Environmental and conservation data

- Forested area as % total land area: 4%
- Protected area as % total land area: 6.2%
- Number of protected areas: 528

SPECIES DIVERSITY

Category	Known species	Threatened species
Mammals	247	42
Breeding birds	304	28
Reptiles	364	19
Amphibians	117	9
Fish	629	29
Plants	23,420	45

Source: World Resources Institute

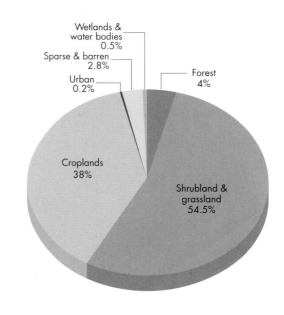

▲ Types of habitat

◄ A humpback whale surfaces off the South African coast. Some 2,000 of these marine mammals pass along the coast as they shuttle between their Antarctic feeding grounds and the warm waters off Mozambique, where they breed.

CHAPTER 14

Future Challenges

The last 30 years have seen a radical transformation in South Africa. Against all the odds, the country has achieved a relatively peaceful transition from apartheid to democracy. However, the dramatic events of the 1990s did not close the gap in living standards between whites and blacks, Coloureds and Asians that was the legacy of apartheid. After the sky-high hopes of the early 1990s, some people inevitably became disillusioned about the rate of progress, and the government's delivery of its promises.

LIFE AFTER APARTHEID

The 1994 government was elected on an immensely ambitious programme. It pledged to provide jobs and improve life for millions of less-privileged citizens, while bringing about reconciliation between races. In the early 2000s, the ANC pursued a cautious but effective economic policy, controlling inflation and creating jobs by encouraging free trade and private investment. The period saw some economic growth, but not enough to significantly reduce unemployment, despite the many thousands of jobs created by the Reconstruction and Development Programme and other initiatives.

Law and order remain a problem. The relaxation of border controls after 1994 has allowed international criminal organizations to

▼ United Nations peacekeepers from South Africa point out a hill that forms a buffer zone between rival army factions fighting in the hills near Kilalo, eastern Congo. The fighting forced thousands to flee. In December 2004, the South African troops helped to secure the buffer zone between the rival groups.

gain a foothold in South Africa, and the country has become a major centre for drug trafficking. The incidence of violent crime (muggings, armed robberies, rape and murder) remains very high, causing wealthy citizens to move from city centres to gated suburbs that provide more security. Meanwhile from the mid-1990s, HIV/AIDS caused a major health crisis, which many feel the government only started to handle effectively in the early 2000s.

HOPES FOR THE FUTURE

Despite these problems, South Africa's economic future looks fairly bright. In the foreseeable future, the country looks set to

? Did you know?

In the early 2000s, half of all government spending went on social services including health and education, but many areas still lack adequate hospitals and schools.

continue as Africa's leading economy. Its strengths include its large mineral reserves such as gold, diamonds and platinum, and also coal, to fuel growing industries. South Africa's well-developed infrastructure will continue to be an important asset. After more than a decade of liberal and stable government, South Africa will continue to play a major role in both African politics and international affairs.

Since 1994, the government has made considerable progress in empowering disadvantaged sectors of the community. In just over ten years, a new black middle class has arisen, but millions, mostly black, still live in poverty. The gulf between the haves and have-nots is still huge, posing a major obstacle to peace and security. After conquering apartheid and giving all races the right to vote, the people of South Africa have made progress in the immense task of equalizing wealth, power and influence in South Africa, but much remains to be done.

▼ A group of boys and girls in Khayelitsha, Cape Town's biggest township. South Africans have cause to be optimistic about the future, although there remain many challenges from the apartheid era.

Timeline

c. 10,000 years ago San Bushmen and Khoekhoen roam South Africa.

c. AD 100 Bantu-speaking Nguni groups move into South Africa.

c. 14th and 15th centuries Sotho, Tswana, Tonga and Venda move into South Africa.

1652 Dutch East India Company founds a settlement at Cape Town.

1806 British take over Cape Colony from the Dutch.

1820-30 Zulus under King Shaka extend their territory, causing other African peoples to flee.

1836 54 The Great Trek: some 16,000 Boers migrate north from the Cape to escape British rule. Dutch Boers found two republics, the Transvaal and Orange Free State.

1840s-1906 British and Boer armies defeat African chiefdoms and take over their lands.

1843 Natal becomes a British colony.

1867 Diamonds are discovered near Kimberley.

1880-1 First Boer War.

1886 Gold is discovered in the Witwatersrand, at what is now Johannesburg.

1899-1902 Second Boer War ends with a British victory.

1906 Last armed black rebellion, the Bambatha Rebellion, is suppressed.

1910 British colonies of Natal and the Cape, and the two Boer republics are united in the Union of South Africa.

1912 African National Congress (ANC) is founded.

1913 Natives' Land Act reserves all but 13 per cent of South Africa for whites.

1923 Native Urban Areas Act restricts blacks to separate areas in cities.

1948 National Party wins power in South Africa and sets up the apartheid system.

1950 Population Registration Act classifies South Africans into four racial groups: blacks, whites, Indians and Coloreds.

1952 Pass Laws require non-whites to carry identity papers at all times.

1960 Sharpeville Massacre. The ANC and allied groups are banned.

1961 *Umkhonto we Sizwe* (MK) commences the armed struggle. South Africa becomes a republic, and is expelled from the British Commonwealth.

1964 Nelson Mandela is sentenced to life imprisonment.

1960s-'70s Bantustan Acts create ten *bantustans* (homelands) for black Africans.

1974 South Africa is expelled from the United Nations.

1976 Soweto Uprising, as Sowetan schoolchildren protest against having their lessons in Afrikaans.

1983 National Party declares a state of emergency.

1986 United States, EEC, and Commonwealth impose trade sanctions on South Africa.

1988 South African army invades Angola and is defeated.

1989 F.W. de Klerk is elected president of the National Party.

1990 ANC is unbanned and Nelson Mandela is released.

1991 Apartheid laws are scrapped.

1994 South Africa holds its first democratic election, with victory for the ANC. Nelson Mandela is elected president. Launch of the Reconstruction and Development Programme.

1996-8 Truth and Reconciliation Commission.

1999 ANC wins a second election victory. Nelson Mandela steps down as president and Thabo Mbeki replaces him.

2003 Government approves major programme to tackle HIV/AIDS.

2004 ANC wins a third election victory.

2005 Vice-president Jacob Zuma leaves office.

2006 Congress of South African Trade Unions (COSATU) calls for a strike to protest against the stalemate at the World Trade Organisation trade talks in Switzerland, aimed at promoting international trade with African nations.

Glossary

Acid rain Rain that is slightly acidic because it is polluted by waste gases from car exhausts and power stations.

Afrikaner A white South African of mainly Dutch descent.

Amnesty A general pardon.

Apartheid The policy of separate development for people of different races that was the South African government's policy between the 1950s and the early 1990s.

Arable land Land on which crops can be grown.

Bantustan A term meaning 'homelands', describing the areas set aside for black Africans to live in during the apartheid era.

Boer Another word for an Afrikaner. The term *boer* means 'farmer' in Afrikaans.

British Commonwealth An organization made up of countries that once formed part of the British Empire.

Coloured The term used in South Africa for people of mixed race, which also includes groups such as the Cape Malays and Khoisan.

Compensation An award, usually of money, paid to someone in recognition that a wrong has been done.

Constitution A set of rules governing a country or organization.

Cyclone A revolving tropical storm, also known as a hurricane.

Democracy A political system in which members of parliament are chosen by people voting in free elections.

Denomination A branch of a particular religion.

Epidemic A major outbreak of disease.

Erosion The wearing away of the land by natural forces such as wind, rain and ice. Erosion is sometimes increased by deforestation or overgrazing by animals.

Ethnic Classification of people according to their racial origins.

Fossil fuel Coal, oil, gas and other fuels formed of fossilized remains of plants or animals that lived millions of years ago.

Fynbos The unique vegetation of the Southwestern Cape region of South Africa, which includes plants such as irises, pelargoniums and proteas. The word means 'fine-leaved bush' in Afrikaans.

Gross Domestic Product (GDP) The total value of the goods and services produced by a country in a year.

Huguenots French Protestants who emigrated to escape persecution in Catholic France in the late 17th century.

Human rights Rights possessed by all people simply because they are human, and deserve to be treated with respect. Human rights include economic, social, and political rights.

Indentured worker A labourer who is bound by a contract of work.

Industrialization The process of developing a country's industries and manufacturing.

Inflation A general increase in prices within a country.

Informal economy The sector of the economy in which employment is unofficial, so employers avoid government regulations and employees avoid paying tax.

Infrastructure The facilities needed for a country to function, including communications and transport.

Judicial Relating to the courts and justice.

Legislative Relating to law and law-making.

Literacy The ability to read and write.

Mineral One of the naturally occurring, non-living substances of which rocks are made.

Plankton The tiny plants and animals that float on the surface of the oceans, and form the base of marine food chains, feeding larger animals of all kinds.

Plateau A flat-topped area of high ground.

Proportional representation A system of electing members of parliament by giving seats to political parties according to their share of the vote in the whole country.

Race Ethnic origin.

Regime A system of government.

Republic A state, or form of government, without a monarch.

Sanctions A ban, usually on trading, also known as a boycott.

Sanitation The provision of sewerage to carry away waste, also standards of public hygiene generally.

Segregation The practice of separating people; in South Africa, according to race.

Squatter camp An illegal shanty town. Squatter camps usually grow up on the edge of cities, without permission from the authorities.

Subsistence farming A type of agriculture in which farmers grow food for their own needs, with little left over to sell for profit.

Tornado A whirlwind, or revolving column of air.

Townships The name given to urban areas that grew up in South Africa on the outskirts of cities or industrial areas during the apartheid era, to house the black workers that staffed the mines, factories or service industries. Unlike squatter camps, these settlements were permitted by the authorities.

Further Information

BOOKS TO READ

Changing Face of South Africa
Rob Bowden, Tony Binns
(Hodder Wayland, 2004)

DK Eyewitness Travel Guides: South Africa
Michael Brett
(Dorling Kindersley, 2003, regularly updated)

Leading Lives: Nelson Mandela
David Downing
(Heinemann Library, 2004)

Country File: South Africa
Ian Graham
(Franklin Watts, 2004)

Nations of the World: South Africa
Jen Green
(Raintree Publishers, 2000)

Insight Guide: South Africa
Jason Mitchell
(Insight Guides, 2003, regularly updated)

Longman History Project: South Africa 1948-1994
the Rise and Fall of Apartheid
Martin Roberts
(Longman, 2001)

AUTOBIOGRAPHY
Long Walk to Freedom
Nelson Mandela
(Time Warner Books, 2000)

USEFUL WEBSITES

http://www.gov.za/
The South African government site, with a wide range of information about all aspects of the country and goverment policy.

http://www.southafrica.net/
South Africa Tourist Board
Official site with details of national parks and a range of other tourist attractions.

http://news.bbc.co.uk/1/hi/world/africa/country_profiles/1071886.stm
BBC news country profile on South Africa.

http://www.africa.upenn.edu/Country_Specific/S_Africa.html
African Studies Center, University of Pennsylvania.

www.cia.gov/cia/publications/factbook/geos/sf.html
The CIA World Factbook, providing up-to-date statistics on South Africa.

http://www.infoplease.com/ipa/A0107983.html
Information about South Africa's geography, economy, government, and people.

Index

Page numbers in **bold** indicate pictures.

About the Author

Dr Jen Green received a doctorate from the University of Sussex (Dept of English and American Studies) in 1982. She worked in publishing for 15 years and is now a full-time writer, who has written over 150 books for children. She lives in Sussex.